Will Shortz Presents

TAME KENKEN

KenKen™: Logic Puzzles That Make You Smarter!

KenKen for Kids

WILL SHORTZ PRESENTS
TAME KENKEN™

200 EASY LOGIC PUZZLES THAT MAKE YOU SMARTER

TETSUYA MIYAMOTO

INTRODUCTION BY
WILL SHORTZ

ST. MARTIN'S GRIFFIN
NEW YORK

www.stmartins.com

ISBN 978-0-312-60513-1

D 10 9 8 7 6 5 4

Introduction

If you consider all the world's greatest puzzle varieties, the ones that have inspired crazes over the years—crosswords, jigsaw puzzles, tangrams, sudoku, etc.—they have several properties in common. They . . .

- Are simple to learn
- Have great depth
- Are variable in difficulty, from easy to hard
- Are mentally soothing and pleasing
- Have some unique feature that makes them different from everything else and instantly addictive

By these standards, a new puzzle called KenKen, the subject of the book you're holding, has the potential to become one of the world's greats.

KenKen is Japanese for "square wisdom" or "cleverness squared." The rules are simple: Fill the grid with digits so as not to repeat a digit in any row or column (as in sudoku) and so the digits within each heavily outlined group of boxes combine to make the arithmetic result indicated.

The simplest KenKen puzzles start with 3×3 boxes and use only addition. Harder examples have larger grids and more arithmetic operations.

KenKen was invented in 2003 by Tetsuya Miyamoto, a Japanese math instructor, as a means to help his students learn arithmetic and develop logical thinking. Tetsuya's education method is unusual. Put simply, he doesn't teach. His philosophy is to make the tools of learning available to students and then let them progress on their own.

Tetsuya's most popular learning tool has been KenKen, which his students spend hours doing and find more engaging than TV and video games.

It's true that KenKen has great capacity for educating and building the mind. But first and foremost it's a puzzle to be enjoyed. It is to numbers what the crossword puzzle is to words.

So turn the page and begin. . . .

—Will Shortz

How to Solve KenKen

KenKen is a logic puzzle with simple rules:

- Fill the grid with digits so as not to repeat a digit in any row or column.
- Digits within each heavily outlined group of squares, called a cage, must combine to make the arithmetic result indicated.
- A 3×3–square puzzle will use the digits from 1 to 3, a 4×4–square puzzle will use the digits from 1 to 4, and so on.

Solving a KenKen puzzle involves pure logic and mathematics. No guesswork is needed. Every puzzle has a unique solution.

In this introductory volume of KenKen, the puzzles use addition and subtraction in the following manner:

- In a cage marked with a plus sign, the given number will be the sum of the digits you enter in the squares.
- In a cage marked with a minus sign, the given number will be the difference between the digits you enter in the squares (the lower digit subtracted from the higher one).

Take the 5 × 5–square example on this page.

9+	4	3+		1−
	8+		1	
2	4−	1−		9+
2−		6+	3	
	2		4−	

To start, fill in the digits in the 1×1 cages—the 4 in the top row, the 1 in the second row, etc. This puzzle has five such isolated squares. They are literally no-brainers.

Next, look for cages whose given numbers are either high or low, since these are often the easiest to solve. For example, the top row has a cage with a sum of 3. The only two digits that add up to 3 are 1 and 2. The 1 can't go in the fourth column, because this column already has a 1. So the 1 must go in the third column. The 2 goes next to it in the fourth column.

Similarly, check out the cage in the first column with a sum of 9. The only two digits from 1 to 5 that add up to 9 are 4 and 5. The 4 can't go in the top row, because this row already has a 4. So it must go in the second row. The 5 goes above it in the first row.

Sometimes the next step in solving a KenKen puzzle is to ignore the given numbers and use sudoku-like logic to avoid repeating a digit in a row or column. For example, the first column in our sample puzzle starts out with 5, 4, and 2. The bottom two squares must be 1 and 3, in some order. (They do indeed have a difference of 2, as shown.) The 3 can't go in the fourth row, because this row already has a 3. So it must go in the fifth row, with the 1 going immediately above it.

Continuing in this way, using these and other techniques left for you to discover, you can work your way around the grid, filling in the rest of the squares. The complete solution is shown here.

Addition and Subtraction Puzzle Tips

In more advanced KenKen puzzles, cages can have more than two squares. It's okay to repeat a digit within a cage, as long as the digit is not repeated in a row or column.

Cages with more than two squares will always involve additions. Subtractions occur only in cages with exactly two squares.

Remember, in doing KenKen, you never have to guess. Every puzzle can be solved by using step-by-step logic. Keep going, and soon you'll be a KenKen master!

Will Shortz Presents

TAME **KENKEN**

+ **1**

1	8+	
5+	1	
	3+	

2 +

5+	3+	
	3	4+
3+		

$+$ **3**

3+	5+	1
		5+
4+		

4 +

3	3+	
6+		
5+		1

3+	**4+**	
	5+	**3+**
3		

6 +

4+	8+	
6+		

$+$ **7**

6+		3
1		3+
5+		

8 +

5+	2	4+
	6+	
1		

+ **9**

1	5+	3+
5+		
	4+	

10 +

4+		5+
3+		
2	4+	

+ **11**

4+		6+
8+		

12 +/−

1−	**4+**	
	1	**5+**
3+		

+/− **13**

3	1−	
3+		5+
2−		

14 +/−

2−		**5+**
3+	**1−**	
		1

+/− **15**

6+		3
2−		5+

16 +/−

5+		**6+**
3		
2−		

+/− **17**

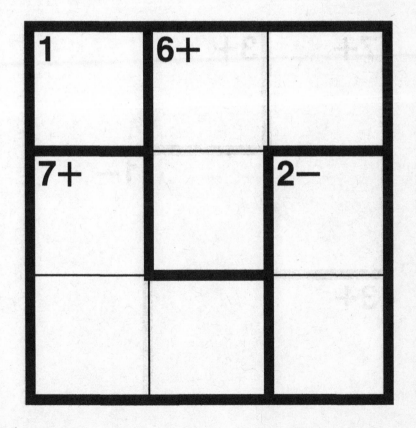

18 +/−

7+	3+	
		1−
3+		

4+		1−
5+		
2	4+	

20 +

7+			5+
5+		6+	
7+	5+		
		5+	

3	3+		7+
3+	1	7+	
	7+		2
4+		3+	

22 +

8+			5+
5+	5+		
		12+	
5+			

+ **23**

7+		3	7+
	5+	3+	
3			7+
5+			

24 +

7+	2	3+	4
	7+		3+
3+		3	
	5+		3

$+$ **25**

3	7+	7+	
7+		1	
	6+		5+
	4+		

26 +

7+	6+		
	4+		9+
3+		11+	

$+$ **27**

3	**7+**	**8+**	**3+**
3+			
	2		**7+**
7+			

28 +

4+	2	7+	
	5+	3+	5+
6+			
	7+		1

+ **29**

3+	7+		5+
	3+	4	
7+		5+	
	3	3+	

30 +

4+	7+		6+
	3+		
6+	4+	3+	
		7+	

+ **31**

3	5+	3+	
5+		2	7+
	2	7+	
5+			1

32 +

6+			9+
3+	1	7+	
	7+		
4		3+	

+ **33**

5+	5+		4
	3+	4+	
5+		4	3+
	7+		

34 +

9+		3+	
	3	5+	
6+	5+		**4**
		5+	

+ **35**

4+		6+	
7+	3+	4+	
		3+	7+
6+			

36 +

7+	8+		
	5+		9+
	8+	3+	

+ **37**

6+		7+	3+
3+	7+		
		4+	
4+		6+	

38 +

9+	6+		
	3+	5+	
		9+	
8+			

+ **39**

5+		3	3+
4	5+	3+	
5+			4
	1	7+	

40 +

3+		12+	
8+	9+		
			5+
	3+		

+ **41**

6+	7+		6+
	4+		
		4+	6+
7+			

42 +

5+		5+	
8+	3+		7+
	5+		
	7+		

+ **43**

5+	5+		4
	5+	5+	
3		5+	3+
5+			

44 +

3+	7+	4+	
		7+	3+
6+			
4+		6+	

+ **45**

5+	5+	6+	
		5+	1
5+	1		7+
	5+		

46 +

1	7+		3+
7+	3	3+	
	3+		7+
2		4	

8+	9+		
	3+	4+	
		3+	7+
6+			

48 +

1	10+	3+	6+
3+		7+	4+
6+			

3+	5+	7+	4
			4+
7+	3+		
	4	3+	

50 +

7+	7+		4+
	3+		
	7+	10+	
			2

+ **51**

6+	5+	3	5+
		3+	
4+			5+
3	6+		

52 +

2	7+		8+
3+			
7+	4+		6+
	3+		

+ **53**

6+		8+	
5+			1
4+	3+		6+
	7+		

54 +

7+		2	6+
	3+	7+	
4			5+
6+			

+ **55**

5+		5+	
6+		1	5+
4+	7+		
	3+		4

56 +

3+	**5+**	**7+**	**1**
			9+
5+		**3+**	
7+			

+ 57

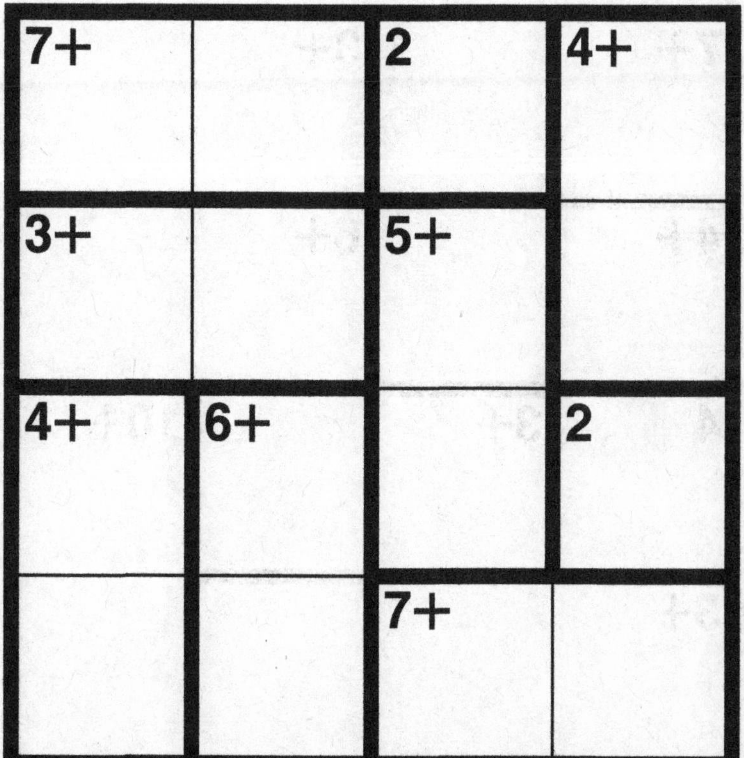

58 +

7+		3+	
4+		6+	
4	3+		10+
3+			

+ **59**

4	4+		3+
5+	3+	7+	
			7+
5+		2	

60 +

7+		**3+**	**6+**
3	**7+**		
		8+	
3+			**3**

+ **61**

7+	3+		7+
	5+	7+	
			3+
7+		1	

62 +

5+	3+		3
	7+		3+
6+		3	
5+		5+	

+ **63**

2	7+		3+
7+	4	4+	
			9+
4+			

64 +/−

6+	**9+**	**1−**	
		7+	
		2−	**4+**
3−			

1−	8+		
	9+		1−
12+			
		3−	

66 +/−

8+			**7**+
7+		**7**+	
6+			
		1−	

68 +/−

1	7+	3	3+
1−		1−	
	3+		4
2		7+	

+/− **69**

3−		12+	
9+	7+		
			1−
	2−		

70 +/−

1−	2−		7+
	9+		
8+			
		5+	

2	7+		4+
7+	1−	1	
		2−	
3−		5+	

72 +/−

7+		6+	1−
3	1−		
3+		10+	
	3−		

7+		**2**	**3−**
6+			
3−	**3+**	**5+**	
		7+	

74 +/−

1	**7+**		**6+**
6+	**4+**	**3+**	
			3
1−		**3−**	

3−	3	2−	
	3−	1−	2−
5+			
	3+		4

76 +/−

5+		**3−**	
3+	**5+**		**1−**
	1−		
7+		**1−**	

2–	3+		7+
	1–	7+	
6+			
	3–		3

78 +/−

3+	7+		1−
	3−		
9+		2−	
	7+		

3−	5+	4+	
		2−	
2−		1−	7+
6+			

80 +/−

7+	11+	1−	
			13+
6+			

3+		1−	4+
7+	2		
	3−		6+
4+		2	

82 +/−

2−		**6+**	
3	**2−**	**4+**	**1−**
2−			
	3−		**3**

+/– **83**

1	7+		3+
2–		3	
5+	3+		7+
	3–		

84 +/−

2−		3−	2
6+			7+
3−	5+	3	
		3+	

2−		6+	
7+		3+	
3+		8+	
4	5+		

86 +/−

3+		**10+**	
9+	**6+**	**4**	
			3+
	3−		

3	3−		3+
2−	1−		
	3+		7+
4+		2	

88 +/−

1−		6+	2−
3−	1		
	7+		2−
2	4+		

7+		3+	
6+		1	1−
4+	3−		
	5+		4

90 +/−

6+			4
7+	7+	2−	
			3+
2	1−		

6+	11+		1−
		4+	
			8+
2−			

92 +/−

1−		11+	
9+	2−		
	3−	3+	
		1−	

7+	3−		5+
	3+	1−	
3+			5+
	7+		

94 +/−

3	1−		7+
3+	9+		
		5+	
4	1−		1

+ **95**

6+	9+		3	8+
		4		
6+	3+		8+	
	5	7+		5+
8+		3+		

96 +

5+	9+			9+
	9+	3+		
9+		1	6+	
	6+	9+	7+	
				2

9+		3+		3
9+			6+	9+
	6+			
2	16+			6+
6+				

98 +

4+	6+		1	10+
	9+			
3+		8+		7+
9+		3+		
8+		6+		1

+ **99**

5+	5+		8+	
	3+	6+		9+
9+		5+		
	9+			1
1	9+		5+	

100 +

6+	9+		3+	
	3	7+	8+	10+
	9+			
		5+		
5	3+		7+	

7+		7+		5+
3+	7+	6+		
		3	11+	
3	3+			8+
9+		3+		

102 +

3+		9+		12+
10+	1	7+		
	7+	3	6+	
				8+
9+				

+ **103**

3+	10+		2	6+
		9+		
17+	3+		9+	
		1	4+	5+
	6+			

104 +

5+	9+		9+	
	4	3+		
9+	3+	7+		7+
		4+		
4+		9+		2

1–		6+	2–	
4	6+		3	3+
2–		1–		
	1–	1	3–	
2		6+		4

106 +/−

1−	4−		1−	12+
	6+	6+		
			10+	
6+				
2−		7+		

1−		8+		4
5	7+		1	1−
4+	9+		2−	
	1−	1		4−
4		3−		

108 +/−

9+		**8+**		**10+**
1−	**6+**			
			12+	
1−	**4−**			
	9+		**1−**	

6+		7+	2	5+
5	1−		6+	
7+		2		6+
	2	4−	4	
1−			1−	

110 +/−

13+		6+		
	6+			9+
1−	3+	4−		
		9+	1−	1−
4−				

1	8+		5+	9+
6+		3+		
8+			3−	
9+	2	5+		5+
	2−		5	

112 +/−

8+	11+			2−
	3−		6+	
1−		3−		11+
4−				
10+				

6+			8+	1−
8+	9+			
	13+			7+
1−		8+		

114 +/−

1	2−		10+	
1−	6+	14+		
			2−	
3−		1−		9+
	2−			

+/− **115**

1−	4+		1−	5
	7+			1−
9+	3−		2	
	9+	4+		3+
3		3−		

116 +/−

4−	3+	6+		3
		7+	9+	
2−	3		2−	5
	9+	1		1−
3		7+		

10+			1–	4–
7+				
12+	6+			1–
	9+	4+		
			3–	

118 +/−

1−		4−		7+
14+	6+		1−	
2−	6+	9+		2−
		1−		

2	4–		11+	
4–		1–		
6+		14+	3	1–
7+				
	6+		4–	

120 +/−

6+		2−		8+
3−		3−		
4−		4	1−	
11+		3+		3−
2		9+		

10+	2	7+	6+	6+
	4−			
		3+	7+	
3−	7+		4−	1−
		5		

122 +/−

9+	3+		7+	4+
	12+			
2		1−	3−	9+
4+	3−			
		2−		2

7+	9+		5+	
	3	4−		
3+	6+	5	4+	1−
		1−		
4−			1−	

124 +/−

4+		12+	3−	
8+			3−	
	1−	8+		6+
			7+	
11+				

11+				2−
2−	4−		4+	
	1−	9+		4−
2−				
	10+			

126 +/−

8+	**9+**		**1−**	
	6+	**2−**	**7+**	
2−			**2−**	**7+**
	4+	**3−**		
1			**9+**	

1	2−		10+	
1−	6+	14+		
			2−	
3−		1−		9+
	2−			

128 +/−

9+		1−	4−	3
3−	3			2−
	8+		2	
1−	2	9+		1
	3−		8+	

1−		**9+**		**1**
2	**4−**	**7+**		**1−**
6+		**3**	**1−**	
	4	**3+**		**5+**
7+			**5**	

130 +/−

6+	4−	7+	10+	
			7+	
5	9+	3+		
4+			4−	
		9+		3

3−		3	3−	
4−		11+	7+	3+
3				
6+	3+		4−	1−
	8+			

132 +/−

12+	5+		3+	6+
	9+			
	3+		3	7+
6+		4−	1−	
4+				2

3	2−		6+	11+
4−	1			
	9+	9+		
		4+	4−	
9+			5+	

134 +/−

12+			**7+**	
5+		**3+**		**13+**
4−	**11+**			
			9+	**1**
2	**4−**			

4−	9+		3	9+
	3+			
1−	6+	5	4−	3−
		4+		
1−			3−	

136 +/−

13+		7+		
7+		10+	3−	4+
	2−		8+	
2−		11+		

6+	3−	11+		
		11+	6+	1−
2−		12+		3+
2−				

138 +/−

4−		8+	2	3−
5+	3		9+	
	5+			3−
3+		1−		
4	3−		4+	

1−		**13+**		**9+**
4+	**8+**		**2−**	
1−		**1−**	**3+**	
7+			**4−**	

140 +/−

13+	5+		4−	
		4+		1−
6+		2−		
1−	3+		9+	
	6+		1−	

6+			**14+**	
1–	**1–**			**4+**
	9+	**1–**		
3+			**1–**	
	4–		**7+**	

142 +/−

1−	9+		3−	
		7+		
8+		3−	11+	
4−				1−
	12+			

3−	4−		12+	2−
	10+	3+		
				9+
10+	8+			
		2−		

144 +/−

2−	**3−**	**8+**		**11+**
		4+		
4+		**8+**		
3−			**10+**	
12+				

9+			7+	
12+	9+			9+
	3+	4+		
		3−		
6+			1−	

146 +/−

8+		3+	4	4−
4	3+		5+	
4+		5		4
	7+		3−	
2	9+		2−	

3−	8+	1−		3−
		5+		
6+		8+		
		2−	1−	
9+			5+	

148 +/−

2	**6+**		**1−**	
4−		**8+**	**2−**	**7+**
12+	**2−**			
			1−	
	1−			**5**

3	13+	3+	3−	
			2−	
3+	1−	9+		7+
		2−	3−	
4−				2

150 +/−

8+			**3−**	
4−	**1−**	**5+**		**6+**
		7+		
7+	**10+**			
		10+		

7+	4−		3	6+
	7+	3+		
4−		9+	5+	8+
	4			
1−			6+	

152 +/−

4	4−		14+	
3+	5+			
	9+		5+	
8+	2−	6+		3−
			4	

9+		7+	4+	
9+			11+	
		14+	1	
4−				7+
	4	3+		

154 +/−

2−		**9+**		**1−**
11+	**2**	**8+**		
	4−	**6+**		**4**
			7+	
7+		**2**	**4−**	

8+	4−		4	6+
	3+	8+		
5+		5		4+
	11+			
9+			4−	

156 +/−

3+		9+		7+
3	8+			
4−	11+		1	7+
		5+		
9+			6+	

4−		9+		4
8+			4−	
4		6+		5+
9+		15+		
3+				

158 +/−

3	9+		4+	3−
5+	2−	4−		
			5+	
2−		5+	10+	
3+				4

9+		4−		4+
8+		4	5+	
	4−			4
	8+	8+		3−
		6+		

160 +/-

1−		7+		2−
7+	11+		4−	
		5+		7+
3−			2−	
	8+			

1−		6+	2−	
4	6+		3	3+
2−		1−		
	1−	1	3−	
2		6+		4

162 +/−

1−		6+		
1−		4−		2−
6+	13+		2−	
	1−			4−
		7+		

4−		9+	2	1−
6+			12+	
	10+			6+
	12+			
		1−		

164 +/−

13+		**7+**		
		9+		**3−**
9+	**4−**			
	3−	**3−**	**2−**	
			4+	

+/− **165**

8+	9+		1−	
	6+	2−	7+	
2−			2−	7+
	4+	3−		
1			9+	

166 +/-

2−		3−		6+
3−	2−	7+		
			4−	
6+	5+		1−	
		10+		

1−		12+	3−	
1−	4−		8+	
			7+	
9+		6+		
1−			3−	

168 +/−

7+	4−	3−		3
		4	3+	
3−	6+	8+		3−
		1−	3	
2−			9+	

6+	9+		2−	
	3−	8+	7+	
			1−	9+
1−	3+			
	1−		3−	

170 +/−

2	8+	3−		5
7+		1	5+	
	6+	7+		3−
4−		3	9+	
	3+			3

11+		8+			11+
5+		7+	11+		
10+				3+	7+
5		10+	6+		
3+				3	9+
8+		3	6+		

172 +

9+	5+		11+		14+
	11+	8+	1		
			9+		3
3+				10+	
10+	6+	5	11+	4+	6+

7+		9+			11+
8+	5+	3+	7+	11+	
					6+
7+		3	7+		
10+	7+		1	6+	4+
	3	11+			

174 +

12+	3+	6+	11+	13+	
	4	3+		13+	
11+		7+		3+	
4+		15+	9+		5
2				5+	

7+		8+		4	9+
13+		1	8+		
	15+		3+		
4+		6+		11+	11+
	7+				
4		11+		4+	

176 +

9+			6+		6
11+	5+		10+		3+
	5+		6+	5+	
6+	11+				7+
	10+	1	16+		
3				6+	

+ **177**

12+		7+	3+	11+	6
					4+
6	6+		8+		
3+		10+	7+	9+	
11+				3+	
8+			6	6+	

178 +

3+		3	10+		14+
5	5+		8+		
7+	4+		9+	3+	
	12+	11+			3+
			3	12+	
11+		3+			

+ **179**

11+	5	3+		11+	
	13+	6+	11+	3+	
4+					3+
		5	9+		
3+		10+		14+	
6+		4+		5	

180 +

12+		7+		9+	
		2	12+	8+	7+
11+	1				
	9+		3+		3
5+	11+		13+		10+
	3+				

5+		**5**	**2−**	**9+**	**8+**
2−		**5−**			
2−	**5−**		**3+**	**7+**	
		9+		**9+**	
11+				**2**	**6+**
2	**1−**		**5−**		

182 +/−

3	5−		11+		
11+	1−	3+	4−		13+
			3−		
7+	11+	3		10+	
		10+		2	
	9+		3	7+	

17+		1	10+		12+
	6+		8+		
		5−		3−	
5−	8+	6+			2−
		8+		4	
9+			5−		5

184 +/−

2−	5−	2	12+	3−	4−
7+		11+	5−	3−	
5−	3−			6+	13+
		8+	3		
5			3+		

1−	7+		5−		4
	14+		7+		5−
11+		1	2−		
	5−	2−	4−	5+	
5+				8+	
	4	5+		1−	

186 +/−

3−	11+		5−		4
		11+	2	9+	
5	5−		11+	3−	
7+					
	4+		6+	21+	
	1−				

8+			5	4−	
3+		12+			14+
4	13+			3+	
10+		1	7+		
8+	1−	4−			3−
			6+		

188 +/−

4	2−		5−		3−
3+		3−	11+	9+	
3−					
4−		3	1−	10+	
14+				5	4+
	11+		5+		

3+	14+	9+		5−	
		4	10+		
4		3+		9+	
12+		3−		3+	
3−		7+		3	13+
		5−			

190 +/−

9+	**8+**		**3−**	**11+**	**8+**
	3+				
	7+		**14+**	**1**	**2−**
11+	**5−**				
	5	**7+**			**3−**
3+		**6**	**8+**		

1−		5−		5	6+
2	14+			5+	
2−		3+			5−
4−		9+		11+	
4−	5−		4		2−
	9+				

192 +/−

3+		5−	12+		
3−			2−		11+
3−		2	9+	3−	
11+	1−				3
		10+		3+	
2	12+			5−	

11+		6+	3+		7+
3+	3		11+		
	2−		6	5+	
2−		11+	9+	7+	
3−	5+			3−	
		1		2−	

194 +/−

3+		3	15+		
2	11+		14+	3−	3+
11+					
	3+		11+		12+
1−	4+			6	
	9+		3+		

2	11+		1−		5−
11+		3+		4−	
	8+		11+		2−
5−	3+			5+	
	3	10+			14+
10+			2		

196 +/−

4	5−		11+	3+	1−
5+	6+	4			
		11+		10+	
8+			8+		10+
1−		4−		3	
4+			10+		

6+		3−		7+	
5+	1−	3+	15+	9+	
					6
5−	13+			6	9+
	5−		2	1−	
5		5+			

198 +/−

10+			11+		
6+	11+	3+	7+	5	5−
				1−	
11+	1	8+			5+
	14+		3+		
2−			6	7+	

8+	3	11+	5−	11+	3+
	2−				
5−		10+	2		1−
	7+			5−	
6+		1	12+		3−
	3+				

200 +/−

8+		5−		6+	
9+	6+		10+		11+
	2	12+			
3+	14+		2−		
		8+		5	
11+			1	9+	

ANSWERS

1

1 **1**	8 **3**	**2**
5 **2**	1 **1**	**3**
3	3 **2**	**1**

2

5 **3**	3 **1**	**2**
2	3 **3**	4 **1**
3 **1**	**2**	**3**

3

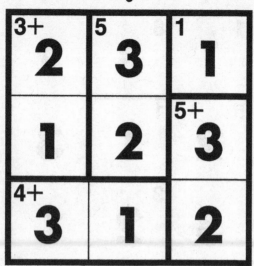

3+ **2**	5 **3**	1 **1**
1	**2**	5+ **3**
4+ **3**	**1**	**2**

4

3 **3**	3+ **1**	**2**
6+ **1**	**2**	**3**
5+ **2**	**3**	1 **1**

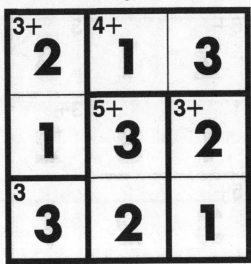

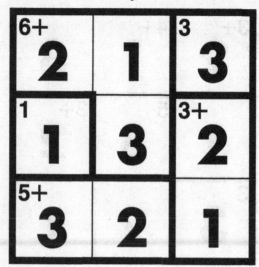

5+ 3	2 2	4+ 1
2	6+ 1	3
1 1	3	2

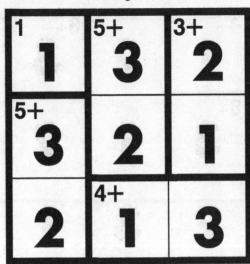

9

11

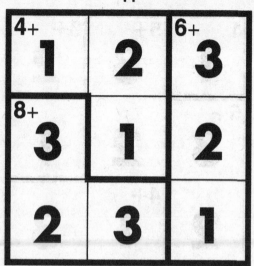

4+ 1	2	6+ 3
8+ 3	1	2
2	3	1

12

1− 2	4+ 3	1
3	1 1	5+ 2
3+ 1	2	3

13

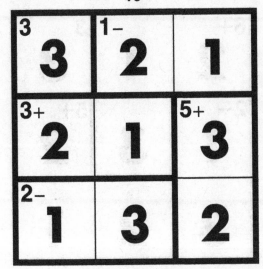

3 **3**	1− **2**	**1**
3+ **2**	**1**	5+ **3**
2− **1**	**3**	**2**

14

2− **3**	**1**	5+ **2**
3+ **1**	1− **2**	**3**
2	**3**	1 **1**

15

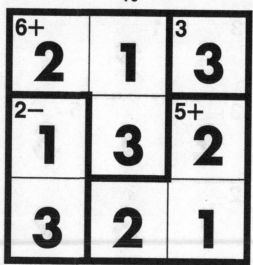

6+ 2	1	3 3
2− 1	3	5+ 2
3	2	1

16

5+ 2	1	6+ 3
3 3	2	1
2− 1	3	2

17

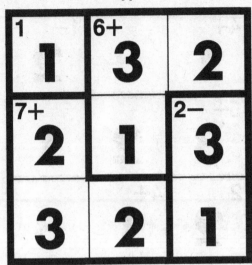

1 **1**	6+ **3**	**2**
2 7+	**1**	2− **3**
3	**2**	**1**

18

7+ **3**	3+ **2**	**1**
1	**3**	1− **2**
3+ **2**	**1**	**3**

19

4+ **1**	**3**	1− **2**
5+ **3**	**2**	**1**
2 **2**	4+ **1**	**3**

20

7+ **2**	**1**	**4**	5+ **3**
5+ **1**	**4**	6+ **3**	**2**
7+ **4**	5+ **3**	**2**	**1**
3	**2**	5+ **1**	**4**

21

3 **3**	3+ **2**	**1**	7+ **4**
3+ **2**	1 **1**	7+ **4**	**3**
1	7+ **4**	**3**	2 **2**
4 **4**	**3**	3+ **2**	**1**

22

8+ **3**	**4**	**1**	5+ **2**
5+ **4**	5+ **1**	**2**	**3**
1	**2**	12+ **3**	**4**
5+ **2**	**3**	**4**	**1**

23

7+ 1	2	**3** 3	**7+** 4
4	**5+** 1	**3+** 2	3
3 3	4	1	**7+** 2
5+ 2	3	4	1

24

7+ 3	**2** 2	**3+** 1	**4** 4
4	**7+** 3	2	**3+** 1
3+ 1	4	**3** 3	2
2	**5+** 1	4	**3** 3

25

³3	⁷4	⁷⁺2	1
⁷⁺2	3	¹1	4
1	⁶⁺2	4	⁵⁺3
4	⁴⁺1	3	2

26

⁷⁺4	⁶⁺3	2	1
3	⁴⁺2	1	⁹⁺4
³⁺2	1	¹¹⁺4	3
1	4	3	2

27

³3	7+4	8+1	3+2
3+2	3	4	1
1	²2	3	7+4
7+4	1	2	3

28

4+1	²2	7+3	4
3	5+4	3+1	5+2
6+4	1	2	3
2	7+3	4	¹1

29

3+ 1	**7+** 4	3	**5+** 2
2	**3+** 1	**4** 4	3
7+ 3	2	**5+** 1	4
4	**3** 3	**3+** 2	1

30

4+ 1	**7+** 4	3	**6+** 2
3	**3+** 2	1	4
6+ 4	**4+** 3	**3+** 2	1
2	1	**7+** 4	3

31

³ 3	⁵⁺ 4	³⁺ 1	2
⁵⁺ 4	1	² 2	⁷⁺ 3
1	² 2	⁷⁺ 3	4
⁵⁺ 2	3	4	¹ 1

32

⁶⁺ 3	2	1	⁹⁺ 4
³⁺ 2	¹ 1	⁷⁺ 4	3
1	⁷⁺ 4	3	2
⁴ 4	3	³⁺ 2	1

33

5+ 1	5+ 3	2	4 4
4	3+ 2	4+ 1	3
5+ 3	1	4 4	3+ 2
2	7+ 4	3	1

34

9+ 3	4	3+ 1	2
2	3 3	5+ 4	1
6+ 1	5+ 2	3	4 4
4	1	5+ 2	3

35

4+ 1	3	**6+** 4	2
7+ 4	**3+** 2	**4+** 3	1
3	1	**3+** 2	**7+** 4
6+ 2	4	1	3

36

7+ 2	**8+** 3	4	1
1	**5+** 2	3	**9+** 4
4	**8+** 1	**3+** 2	3
3	4	1	2

37

6+ 4	2	7+ 3	3+ 1
3+ 1	7+ 3	4	2
2	4	4+ 1	3
4+ 3	1	6+ 2	4

38

9+ 4	6+ 3	2	1
3	3+ 2	5+ 1	4
2	1	9+ 4	3
8+ 1	4	3	2

39

5+ 1	4	**3** 3	**3+** 2
4 4	**5+** 3	**3+** 2	1
5+ 3	2	1	**4** 4
2	**1** 1	**7+** 4	3

40

3+ 2	1	**12+** 4	3
8+ 1	**9+** 4	3	2
4	3	2	**5+** 1
3	**3+** 2	1	4

41

6+ 2	**7+** 3	4	**6+** 1
4	**4+** 1	2	3
1	2	**4+** 3	**6+** 4
7+ 3	4	1	2

42

5+ 2	3	**5+** 4	1
8+ 4	**3+** 1	2	**7+** 3
1	**5+** 2	3	4
3	**7+** 4	1	2

43

5+ 1	5+ 2	3	4 4
4	5+ 1	5+ 2	3
3 3	4	5+ 1	3+ 2
5+ 2	3	4	1

44

3+ 2	7+ 4	4+ 1	3
1	3	7+ 4	3+ 2
6+ 4	2	3	1
4+ 3	1	6+ 2	4

45

5+ 1	5+ 3	6+ 4	2
4	2	5+ 3	1 1
5+ 3	1 1	2	7+ 4
2	5+ 4	1	3

46

1 1	7+ 4	3	3+ 2
7+ 4	3 3	3+ 2	1
3	3+ 2	1	7+ 4
2 2	1	4 4	3

47

8+ 1	**9+** 3	4	2
4	**3+** 2	**4+** 3	1
3	1	**3+** 2	**7+** 4
6+ 2	4	1	3

48

1 1	**10+** 3	**3+** 2	**6+** 4
3	4	1	2
3+ 2	1	**7+** 4	**4+** 3
6+ 4	2	3	1

49

3+ 1	**5+** 2	**7+** 3	**4** 4
2	3	4	**4+** 1
7+ 4	**3+** 1	2	3
3	**4** 4	**3+** 1	2

50

7+ 2	**7+** 4	3	**4+** 1
4	**3+** 2	1	3
1	**7+** 3	**10+** 2	4
3	1	4	**2** 2

51

6+ 4	**5+** 1	**3** 3	**5+** 2
2	4	**3+** 1	3
4+ 1	3	2	**5+** 4
3 3	**6+** 2	4	1

52

2 2	**7+** 4	3	**8+** 1
3+ 1	2	4	3
7+ 4	**4+** 3	1	**6+** 2
3	**3+** 1	2	4

53

6+ 4	2	**8+** 1	3
5+ 2	3	4	**1** 1
4+ 3	**3+** 1	2	**6+** 4
1	**7+** 4	3	2

54

7+ 1	3	**2** 2	**6+** 4
3	**3+** 1	**7+** 4	2
4 4	2	3	**5+** 1
6+ 2	4	1	3

55

5+ 2	3	**5+** 4	1
6+ 4	2	**1** 1	**5+** 3
4+ 1	**7+** 4	3	2
3	**3+** 1	2	**4** 4

56

3+ 2	**5+** 3	**7+** 4	**1** 1
1	2	3	**9+** 4
5+ 4	1	**3+** 2	3
7+ 3	4	1	2

57

7+ 4	3	2️ 2	4+ 1
3+ 2	1	5+ 4	3
4+ 3	6+ 4	1	2️ 2
1	2	7+ 3	4

58

7+ 3	4	3+ 2	1
4+ 1	3	6+ 4	2
4️ 4	3+ 2	1	10+ 3
3+ 2	1	3	4

59

4 **4**	4+ **3**	**1**	3+ **2**
5+ **3**	3+ **2**	7+ **4**	**1**
2	**1**	**3**	7+ **4**
5+ **1**	**4**	2 **2**	**3**

60

7+ **4**	**3**	3+ **1**	6+ **2**
3 **3**	7+ **1**	**2**	**4**
2	**4**	8+ **3**	**1**
3+ **1**	**2**	**4**	3 **3**

61

7+ 4	**3+** 1	2	**7+** 3
1	**5+** 2	**7+** 3	4
2	3	4	**3+** 1
7+ 3	4	**1** 1	2

62

5+ 4	**3+** 1	2	**3** 3
1	**7+** 3	4	**3+** 2
6+ 2	4	**3** 3	1
5+ 3	2	**5+** 1	4

63

2 2	**7+** 3	4	**3+** 1
7+ 1	**4** 4	**4+** 3	2
4	2	1	**9+** 3
4+ 3	1	2	4

64

6+ 3	**9+** 4	**1−** 1	2
1	2	**7+** 3	4
2	3	**2−** 4	**4+** 1
3− 4	1	2	3

65

2 (1−)	1 (8+)	4	3
1	4 (9+)	3	2 (1−)
4 (12+)	3	2	1
3	2	1 (3−)	4

66

3 (1−)	4	1 (6+)	2
4 (3−)	1	2	3 (8+)
1	2 (7+)	3 (1−)	4
2	3	4	1

8+ 3	4	1	**7+** 2
7+ 2	3	**7+** 4	1
6+ 1	2	3	4
4	1	**1−** 2	3

1 1	**7+** 4	**3** 3	**3+** 2
1− 4	3	**1−** 2	1
3	**3+** 2	1	**4** 4
2 2	1	**7+** 4	3

69

3− 1	4	**12+** 2	3
9+ 2	**7+** 1	3	4
3	2	4	**1−** 1
4	**2−** 3	1	2

70

1− 4	**2−** 3	1	**7+** 2
3	**9+** 2	4	1
8+ 2	1	3	4
1	4	**5+** 2	3

71

²**2**	⁷⁺**3**	**4**	⁴⁺**1**
⁷⁺**4**	^{1−}**2**	¹**1**	**3**
3	**1**	^{2−}**2**	**4**
^{3−}**1**	**4**	⁵⁺**3**	**2**

72

⁷⁺**4**	**3**	⁶⁺**2**	^{1−}**1**
³**3**	^{1−}**1**	**4**	**2**
³⁺**1**	**2**	¹⁰⁺**3**	**4**
2	^{3−}**4**	**1**	**3**

73

7+ 3	4	**2** 2	**3−** 1
6+ 2	3	1	4
3− 4	**3+** 1	**5+** 3	2
1	2	**7+** 4	3

74

1 1	**7+** 4	3	**6+** 2
6+ 2	**4+** 3	**3+** 1	4
4	1	2	**3** 3
1− 3	2	**3−** 4	1

75

1 ^(3−)	**3** ^(3)	**4** ^(2−)	**2**
4	**1** ^(3−)	**2** ^(1−)	**3** ^(2−)
2 ^(5+)	**4**	**3**	**1**
3	**2** ^(3+)	**1**	**4** ^(4)

76

3 ^(5+)	**2**	**1** ^(3−)	**4**
2 ^(3+)	**1** ^(5+)	**4**	**3** ^(1−)
1	**4** ^(1−)	**3**	**2**
4 ^(7+)	**3**	**2** ^(1−)	**1**

77

2− **3**	3+ **1**	**2**	7+ **4**
1	1− **3**	7+ **4**	**2**
6+ **4**	**2**	**3**	**1**
2	3− **4**	**1**	3 **3**

78

3+ **1**	7+ **3**	**4**	1− **2**
2	3− **4**	**1**	**3**
9+ **4**	**2**	2− **3**	**1**
3	7+ **1**	**2**	**4**

3− 4	**5+** 2	**4+** 3	1
1	3	**2−** 4	2
2− 3	1	**1−** 2	**7+** 4
6+ 2	4	1	3

7+ 4	**11+** 3	**1−** 2	1
1	4	3	**13+** 2
2	1	4	3
6+ 3	2	1	4

81

3+ 2	1	**1−** 4	**4+** 3
7+ 4	**2** 2	3	1
3	**3−** 4	1	**6+** 2
4+ 1	3	**2** 2	4

82

2− 1	3	**6+** 2	4
3 3	**2−** 4	**4+** 1	**1−** 2
2− 4	2	3	1
2	**3−** 1	4	**3** 3

83

1 **1**	7+ **3**	**4**	3+ **2**
2− **4**	**2**	3 **3**	**1**
5+ **3**	3+ **1**	**2**	7+ **4**
2	3− **4**	**1**	**3**

84

2− **3**	**1**	3− **4**	2 **2**
6+ **2**	**4**	**1**	7+ **3**
3− **1**	5+ **2**	3 **3**	**4**
4	**3**	3+ **2**	**1**

85

2− 1	3	**6+** 2	4
7+ 3	4	**3+** 1	2
3+ 2	1	**8+** 4	3
4 4	**5+** 2	3	1

86

3+ 1	2	**10+** 3	4
9+ 2	**6+** 1	**4** 4	3
4	3	2	**3+** 1
3	**3−** 4	1	2

87

³3	³⁻1	4	³⁺2
²⁻2	¹⁻4	3	1
4	³⁺2	1	⁷⁺3
⁴⁺1	3	²2	4

88

¹⁻3	2	⁶⁺4	²⁻1
³⁻4	¹1	2	3
1	⁷⁺4	3	²⁻2
²2	⁴⁺3	1	4

89

7+ 4	3	3+ 2	1
6+ 2	4	1 1	1− 3
4+ 3	3− 1	4	2
1	5+ 2	3	4 4

90

6+ 1	3	2	4 4
7+ 4	7+ 2	2− 1	3
3	1	4	3+ 2
2 2	1− 4	3	1

91

6+ 1	11+ 3	4	1- 2
2	4	4+ 1	3
3	1	2	8+ 4
2- 4	2	3	1

92

1- 1	2	11+ 4	3
9+ 2	2- 3	1	4
3	3- 4	3+ 2	1
4	1	1- 3	2

93

7+ 3	**3−** 4	1	**5+** 2
4	**3+** 1	**1−** 2	3
3+ 1	2	3	**5+** 4
2	**7+** 3	4	1

94

3 3	**1−** 2	1	**7+** 4
3+ 2	**9+** 1	4	3
1	4	**5+** 3	2
4 4	**1−** 3	2	**1** 1

95

6+ 1	9+ 4	5	3 3	8+ 2
3	2	4 4	1	5
6+ 4	3+ 1	2	8+ 5	3
2	5 5	7+ 3	4	5+ 1
8+ 5	3	3+ 1	2	4

96

5+ 2	9+ 1	3	5	9+ 4
3	9+ 4	3+ 2	1	5
9+ 4	5	1 1	6+ 2	3
5	6+ 2	9+ 4	7+ 3	1
1	3	5	4	2 2

97

9+ 4	5	**3+** 1	2	**3** 3
9+ 1	2	3	**6+** 5	**9+** 4
3	**6+** 4	2	1	5
2 2	**16+** 3	5	4	**6+** 1
6+ 5	1	4	3	2

98

4+ 3	**6+** 2	4	**1** 1	**10+** 5
1	**9+** 4	5	3	2
3+ 2	1	**8+** 3	5	**7+** 4
9+ 4	5	**3+** 1	2	3
8+ 5	3	**6+** 2	4	**1** 1

99

5+ 2	5+ 4	1	8+ 5	3
3	3+ 2	6+ 5	1	9+ 4
9+ 4	1	5+ 3	2	5
5	9+ 3	2	4	1 1
1 1	9+ 5	4	5+ 3	2

100

6+ 3	9+ 5	4	3+ 1	2
1	3 3	7+ 2	8+ 5	10+ 4
2	9+ 4	5	3	1
4	1	5+ 3	2	5
5 5	3+ 2	1	7+ 4	3

101

7+ 5	2	7+ 4	3	5+ 1
3+ 2	7+ 3	6+ 5	1	4
1	4	3 3	11+ 5	2
3 3	3+ 1	2	4	8+ 5
9+ 4	5	3+ 1	2	3

102

3+ 1	2	9+ 4	5	12+ 3
10+ 3	1 1	7+ 5	2	4
2	7+ 4	3 3	6+ 1	5
5	3	1	4	8+ 2
9+ 4	5	2	3	1

103

3+ 1	10+ 4	3	2 2	6+ 5
2	3	9+ 5	4	1
17+ 3	3+ 1	2	9+ 5	4
4	5	1 1	4+ 3	5+ 2
5	6+ 2	4	1	3

104

5+ 2	9+ 5	4	9+ 3	1
3	4 4	3+ 1	2	5
9+ 4	3+ 1	7+ 2	5	7+ 3
5	2	4+ 3	1	4
4+ 1	3	9+ 5	4	2 2

105

1− **1**	**2**	6+ **4**	2− **5**	**3**
4 **4**	6+ **5**	**2**	3 **3**	3+ **1**
2− **5**	**1**	1− **3**	**4**	**2**
3	1− **4**	1 **1**	3− **2**	**5**
2 **2**	**3**	6+ **5**	**1**	4 **4**

106

1− **4**	4− **1**	**5**	1− **2**	12+ **3**
5	6+ **2**	6+ **1**	**3**	**4**
1	**3**	**2**	10+ **4**	**5**
6+ **2**	**4**	**3**	**5**	**1**
2− **3**	**5**	7+ **4**	**1**	**2**

107

^{1−}**2**	**1**	⁸⁺**5**	**3**	⁴**4**
⁵**5**	⁷⁺**4**	**3**	¹**1**	^{1−}**2**
⁴⁺**1**	⁹⁺**5**	**4**	^{2−}**2**	**3**
3	^{1−}**2**	¹**1**	**4**	^{4−}**5**
⁴**4**	**3**	^{3−}**2**	**5**	**1**

108

⁹⁺**5**	**4**	⁸⁺**3**	**2**	¹⁰⁺**1**
^{1−}**4**	⁶⁺**3**	**2**	**1**	**5**
3	**2**	**1**	¹²⁺**5**	**4**
^{1−}**2**	^{4−}**1**	**5**	**4**	**3**
1	⁹⁺**5**	**4**	^{1−}**3**	**2**

109

6+ 1	5	7+ 4	2 2	5+ 3
5 5	1- 4	3	6+ 1	2
7+ 4	3	2 2	5	6+ 1
3	2 2	4- 1	4 4	5
1- 2	1	5	1- 3	4

110

13+ 5	4	6+ 3	2	1
4	6+ 3	2	1	9+ 5
1- 3	3+ 2	4- 1	5	4
2	1	9+ 5	1- 4	1- 3
4- 1	5	4	3	2

111

1^1	**3**^8+	**5**	**2**^5+	**4**^9+
2^6+	**4**	**1**^3+	**3**	**5**
3^8+	**5**	**2**	**4**^3−	**1**
5^9+	**2**^2	**4**^5+	**1**	**3**^5+
4	**1**^2−	**3**	**5**^5	**2**

112

3^8+	**2**^11+	**4**	**5**	**1**^2−
5	**4**^3−	**1**	**2**^6+	**3**
4^1−	**3**	**5**^3−	**1**	**2**^11+
1^4−	**5**	**2**	**3**	**4**
2^10+	**1**	**3**	**4**	**5**

113

6+ 3	2	1	8+ 4	1- 5
8+ 2	9+ 1	5	3	4
5	13+ 4	3	1	7+ 2
1	5	4	2	3
1- 4	3	8+ 2	5	1

114

1 1	2- 4	2	10+ 3	5
1- 3	6+ 1	14+ 4	5	2
4	2	5	2- 1	3
3- 5	3	1- 1	2	9+ 4
2	2- 5	3	4	1

115

1− **2**	4+ **3**	**1**	1− **4**	5 **5**
1	7+ **2**	**5**	**3**	1− **4**
9+ **5**	3− **1**	**4**	2 **2**	**3**
4	9+ **5**	4+ **3**	**1**	3+ **2**
3 **3**	**4**	3− **2**	**5**	**1**

116

4− **5**	3+ **1**	6+ **2**	**4**	3 **3**
1	**2**	7+ **3**	9+ **5**	**4**
2− **2**	3 **3**	**4**	2− **1**	5 **5**
4	9+ **5**	1 **1**	**3**	1− **2**
3 **3**	**4**	7+ **5**	**2**	**1**

117

10+ 2	3	5	1- 4	4- 1
7+ 1	2	4	3	5
12+ 5	6+ 1	3	2	1- 4
4	9+ 5	4+ 2	1	3
3	4	1	3- 5	2

118

1- 2	3	4- 5	1	7+ 4
14+ 5	6+ 1	3	1- 4	2
4	5	2	3	1
2- 1	6+ 2	9+ 4	5	2- 3
3	4	1- 1	2	5

119

²**2**	^{4−}**5**	**1**	¹¹⁺**4**	**3**
^{4−}**5**	**1**	^{1−}**3**	**2**	**4**
⁶⁺**4**	**2**	¹⁴⁺**5**	³**3**	^{1−}**1**
⁷⁺**1**	**3**	**4**	**5**	**2**
3	⁶⁺**4**	**2**	^{4−}**1**	**5**

120

⁶⁺**4**	**2**	^{2−}**3**	**1**	⁸⁺**5**
^{3−}**1**	**4**	^{3−}**2**	**5**	**3**
^{4−}**5**	**1**	⁴**4**	^{1−}**3**	**2**
¹¹⁺**3**	**5**	³⁺**1**	**2**	^{3−}**4**
²**2**	**3**	⁹⁺**5**	**4**	**1**

121

10+ 5	2 2	7+ 3	6+ 4	6+ 1
3	4− 1	4	2	5
2	5	3+ 1	7+ 3	4
3− 1	7+ 4	2	4− 5	1− 3
4	3	5 5	1	2

122

9+ 4	3+ 2	1	7+ 5	4+ 3
5	12+ 3	4	2	1
2 2	5	1− 3	3− 1	9+ 4
4+ 3	3− 1	2	4	5
1	4	2− 5	3	2 2

123

7+ 3	**9+** 5	4	**5+** 2	1
4	**3** 3	**4−** 1	5	2
3+ 1	**6+** 2	**5** 5	**4+** 3	**1−** 4
2	4	**1−** 3	1	5
4− 5	1	2	**1−** 4	3

124

4+ 3	1	**12+** 4	**3−** 2	5
8+ 2	5	3	**3−** 1	4
1	**1−** 4	**8+** 2	5	**6+** 3
5	3	1	**7+** 4	2
11+ 4	2	5	3	1

125

11+ 1	3	2	5	2− 4
2− 4	4− 1	5	4+ 3	2
2	1− 4	9+ 3	1	4− 5
2− 3	5	4	2	1
5	10+ 2	1	4	3

126

8+ 3	9+ 5	4	1− 2	1
5	6+ 2	2− 1	7+ 4	3
2− 2	4	3	2− 1	7+ 5
4	4+ 1	3− 5	3	2
1 1	3	2	9+ 5	4

127

1 **1**	2- **4**	**2**	10+ **3**	**5**
1- **3**	6+ **1**	14+ **4**	**5**	**2**
4	**2**	**5**	2- **1**	**3**
3- **5**	**3**	1- **1**	**2**	9+ **4**
2	2- **5**	**3**	**4**	**1**

128

9+ **5**	**4**	1- **2**	4- **1**	3 **3**
3- **4**	3 **3**	**1**	**5**	2- **2**
1	8+ **5**	**3**	2 **2**	**4**
1- **3**	2 **2**	9+ **5**	**4**	1 **1**
2	3- **1**	**4**	8+ **3**	**5**

129

1− **3**	**2**	9+ **5**	**4**	1 **1**
2 **2**	4− **1**	7+ **4**	**3**	1− **5**
6+ **1**	**5**	3 **3**	1− **2**	**4**
5	4 **4**	3+ **2**	**1**	5+ **3**
7+ **4**	**3**	**1**	5 **5**	**2**

130

6+ **2**	4− **1**	7+ **4**	10+ **3**	**5**
4	**5**	**3**	7+ **1**	**2**
5 **5**	9+ **3**	3+ **1**	**2**	**4**
4+ **3**	**4**	**2**	4− **5**	**1**
1	**2**	9+ **5**	**4**	3 **3**

131

3− 1	4	3 3	3− 2	5
4− 5	1	11+ 4	7+ 3	3+ 2
3 3	5	2	4	1
6+ 4	3+ 2	1	4− 5	1− 3
2	8+ 3	5	1	4

132

12+ 4	5+ 2	3	3+ 1	6+ 5
3	9+ 5	4	2	1
5	3+ 1	2	3 3	7+ 4
6+ 2	4	4− 1	1− 5	3
4+ 1	3	5	4	2 2

133

3 **3**	2− **2**	**4**	6+ **1**	11+ **5**
4− **5**	1 **1**	**2**	**3**	**4**
1	9+ **3**	9+ **5**	**4**	**2**
2	**4**	4+ **3**	4− **5**	**1**
9+ **4**	**5**	**1**	5+ **2**	**3**

134

12+ **4**	**5**	**3**	7+ **1**	**2**
5+ **3**	**2**	3+ **1**	**4**	13+ **5**
4− **1**	11+ **4**	**2**	**5**	**3**
5	**3**	**4**	9+ **2**	1 **1**
2 **2**	4− **1**	**5**	**3**	**4**

135

4− **1**	9+ **5**	**4**	3 **3**	9+ **2**
5	3+ **1**	**2**	**4**	**3**
1− **3**	6+ **2**	5 **5**	4− **1**	3− **4**
2	**4**	4+ **3**	**5**	**1**
1− **4**	**3**	**1**	3− **2**	**5**

136

13+ **5**	**3**	7+ **1**	**2**	**4**
7+ **2**	**5**	10+ **3**	3− **4**	4+ **1**
4	**2**	**5**	**1**	**3**
1	2− **4**	**2**	8+ **3**	**5**
2− **3**	**1**	11+ **4**	**5**	**2**

137

⁶⁺3	^{3−}1	¹¹⁺2	4	5
1	4	¹¹⁺5	⁶⁺2	^{1−}3
2	5	1	3	4
^{2−}5	3	¹²⁺4	1	³⁺2
^{2−}4	2	3	5	1

138

^{4−}5	1	⁸⁺3	²2	^{3−}4
⁵⁺2	³3	5	⁹⁺4	1
3	⁵⁺4	1	5	^{3−}2
³⁺1	2	^{1−}4	3	5
⁴4	^{3−}5	2	⁴⁺1	3

139

1− 2	1	**13+** 5	4	**9+** 3
4+ 1	**8+** 5	4	**2−** 3	2
3	2	1	5	4
1− 5	4	**1−** 3	**3+** 2	1
7+ 4	3	2	**4−** 1	5

140

13+ 4	**5+** 3	2	**4−** 5	1
5	4	**4+** 3	1	**1−** 2
6+ 1	5	**2−** 4	2	3
1− 3	**3+** 2	1	**9+** 4	5
2	**6+** 1	5	**1−** 3	4

141

6+ 3	2	1	**14+** 4	5
1− 4	**1−** 3	2	5	**4+** 1
5	**9+** 4	**1−** 3	1	2
3+ 1	5	4	**1−** 2	3
2	**4−** 1	5	**7+** 3	4

142

1− 4	**9+** 1	3	**3−** 2	5
3	5	**7+** 2	1	4
8+ 2	4	**3−** 1	**11+** 5	3
4− 5	2	4	3	**1−** 1
1	**12+** 3	5	4	2

143

3− 4	4− 1	5	12+ 3	2− 2
1	10+ 3	3+ 2	5	4
5	2	1	4	9+ 3
10+ 2	8+ 4	3	1	5
3	5	2− 4	2	1

144

2− 4	3− 1	8+ 5	3	11+ 2
2	4	4+ 3	1	5
4+ 1	3	8+ 2	5	4
3− 5	2	1	10+ 4	3
12+ 3	5	4	2	1

145

9+ 2	4	3	7+ 5	1
12+ 3	9+ 5	4	1	9+ 2
5	3+ 2	4+ 1	3	4
4	1	3- 5	2	3
6+ 1	3	2	1- 4	5

146

8+ 5	3	3+ 2	4 4	4- 1
4 4	3+ 2	1	5+ 3	5
4+ 3	1	5 5	2	4 4
1	7+ 4	3	3- 5	2
2 2	9+ 5	4	2- 1	3

147

3− 2	**8+** 3	**1−** 4	5	**3−** 1
5	1	**5+** 2	3	4
6+ 3	4	**8+** 5	1	2
1	2	**2−** 3	**1−** 4	5
9+ 4	5	1	**5+** 2	3

148

2 2	**6+** 1	5	**1−** 4	3
4− 1	5	**8+** 4	**2−** 3	**7+** 2
12+ 3	**2−** 2	1	5	4
5	4	3	**1−** 2	1
4	**1−** 3	2	1	**5** 5

149

³3	¹³⁺4	³⁺1	³⁻2	5
4	5	2	²⁻3	1
³⁺1	¹⁻2	⁹⁺4	5	⁷⁺3
2	3	²⁻5	³⁻1	4
⁴⁻5	1	3	4	²2

150

⁸⁺4	3	1	³⁻2	5
⁴⁻5	¹⁻4	⁵⁺2	3	⁶⁺1
1	5	⁷⁺3	4	2
⁷⁺2	¹⁰⁺1	4	5	3
3	2	¹⁰⁺5	1	4

151

7+ **4**	4− **1**	**5**	3 **3**	6+ **2**
3	7+ **5**	3+ **1**	**2**	**4**
4− **1**	**2**	9+ **3**	5+ **4**	8+ **5**
5	4 **4**	**2**	**1**	**3**
1− **2**	**3**	**4**	6+ **5**	**1**

152

4 **4**	4− **5**	**1**	14+ **2**	**3**
3+ **1**	5+ **2**	**3**	**5**	**4**
2	9+ **4**	**5**	5+ **3**	**1**
8+ **5**	2− **3**	6+ **4**	**1**	3− **2**
3	**1**	**2**	4 **4**	**5**

153

9+ 4	5	**7+** 2	**4+** 3	1
9+ 3	1	5	**11+** 4	2
2	3	**14+** 4	**1** 1	5
4− 1	2	3	5	**7+** 4
5	**4** 4	**3+** 1	2	3

154

2− 1	3	**9+** 4	5	**1−** 2
11+ 4	**2** 2	**8+** 5	3	1
5	**4−** 1	**6+** 3	2	**4** 4
2	5	1	**7+** 4	3
7+ 3	4	**2** 2	**4−** 1	5

155

8+ 3	4− 5	1	4 4	6+ 2
5	3+ 1	8+ 3	2	4
5+ 4	2	5 5	3	4+ 1
1	11+ 4	2	5	3
9+ 2	3	4	4− 1	5

156

3+ 2	1	9+ 5	4	7+ 3
3 3	8+ 5	1	2	4
4− 5	11+ 3	4	1 1	7+ 2
1	4	5+ 2	3	5
9+ 4	2	3	6+ 5	1

157

4− 1	5	**9+** 2	3	**4** 4
8+ 3	2	4	**4−** 1	5
4 4	3	**6+** 1	5	**5+** 2
9+ 5	4	**15+** 3	2	1
3+ 2	1	5	4	3

158

3 3	**9+** 5	4	**4+** 1	**3−** 2
5+ 4	**2−** 2	**4−** 1	3	5
1	4	5	**5+** 2	3
2− 5	3	**5+** 2	**10+** 4	1
3+ 2	1	3	5	**4** 4

159

9+ 4	2	4− 5	1	4+ 3
8+ 5	3	4 4	5+ 2	1
2	4− 5	1	3	4 4
1	8+ 4	8+ 3	5	3− 2
3	1	6+ 2	4	5

160

1− 1	2	7+ 4	3	2− 5
7+ 4	11+ 5	2	4− 1	3
3	4	5+ 1	5	7+ 2
3− 5	1	3	2− 2	4
2	8+ 3	5	4	1

161

1− **1**	**2**	6+ **4**	2− **5**	**3**
4 **4**	6+ **5**	**2**	3 **3**	3+ **1**
2− **5**	**1**	1− **3**	**4**	**2**
3	1− **4**	1 **1**	3− **2**	**5**
2 **2**	**3**	6+ **5**	**1**	4 **4**

162

1− **5**	**4**	6+ **2**	**1**	**3**
1− **4**	**3**	4− **1**	**5**	2− **2**
6+ **1**	13+ **5**	**3**	2− **2**	**4**
3	1− **2**	**5**	**4**	4− **1**
2	**1**	7+ **4**	**3**	**5**

163

4− 5	1	9+ 3	2 2	1− 4
6+ 1	2	4	12+ 3	5
3	10+ 4	1	5	6+ 2
2	12+ 3	5	4	1
4	5	1− 2	1	3

164

13+ 5	3	7+ 2	1	4
1	4	9+ 3	2	3− 5
9+ 3	4− 1	5	4	2
4	3− 2	3− 1	2− 5	3
2	5	4	4+ 3	1

165

8+ 3	**9+** 5	4	**1−** 2	1
5	**6+** 2	**2−** 1	**7+** 4	3
2− 2	4	3	**2−** 1	**7+** 5
4	**4+** 1	**3−** 5	3	2
1 1	3	2	**9+** 5	4

166

2− 3	5	**3−** 4	1	**6+** 2
3− 5	**2−** 2	**7+** 1	3	4
2	4	3	**4−** 5	1
6+ 1	**5+** 3	2	**1−** 4	5
4	1	**10+** 5	2	3

167

1− 3	2	12+ 5	3− 1	4
1− 2	4− 1	4	8+ 5	3
1	5	3	7+ 4	2
9+ 5	4	6+ 2	3	1
1− 4	3	1	3− 2	5

168

7+ 4	4− 1	3− 5	2	3 3
3	5	4 4	3+ 1	2
3− 2	6+ 4	8+ 3	5	3− 1
5	2	1− 1	3 3	4
2− 1	3	2	9+ 4	5

169

6+ 2	9+ 5	4	2- 1	3
1	3- 4	8+ 3	7+ 5	2
3	1	5	1- 2	9+ 4
1- 4	3+ 2	1	3	5
5	1- 3	2	3- 4	1

170

2 2	8+ 3	3- 4	1	5 5
7+ 4	5	1 1	5+ 3	2
3	6+ 4	7+ 5	2	3- 1
4- 1	2	3 3	9+ 5	4
5	3+ 1	2	4	3 3

171

11+ 6	5	**8+** 1	3	4	**11+** 2
5+ 4	1	**7+** 2	**11+** 5	6	3
10+ 3	4	5	6	**3+** 2	**7+** 1
5 5	3	**10+** 4	**6+** 2	1	6
3+ 1	2	6	4	**3** 3	**9+** 5
8+ 2	6	**3** 3	**6+** 1	5	4

172

9+ 1	**5+** 3	2	**11+** 6	5	**14+** 4
3	**11+** 5	**8+** 4	**1** 1	6	2
5	6	1	**9+** 4	2	**3** 3
3+ 2	1	3	5	**10+** 4	6
10+ 6	**6+** 4	**5** 5	**11+** 2	**4+** 3	**6+** 1
4	2	6	3	1	5

173

7+ 1	6	9+ 4	2	3	11+ 5
8+ 3	5+ 1	3+ 2	7+ 4	11+ 5	6
5	4	1	3	6	6+ 2
7+ 2	5	3 3	7+ 6	1	4
10+ 6	7+ 2	5	1 1	6+ 4	4+ 3
4	3 3	11+ 6	5	2	1

174

12+ 4	3+ 1	6+ 5	11+ 2	13+ 6	3
5	2	1	6	3	4
3	4 4	3+ 2	1	13+ 5	6
11+ 6	5	7+ 4	3	3+ 1	2
4+ 1	3	15+ 6	9+ 4	2	5 5
2 2	6	3	5	5+ 4	1

175

7+ 6	1	8+ 3	5	4 4	9+ 2
13+ 2	6	1 1	8+ 3	5	4
5	15+ 4	6	3+ 1	2	3
4+ 3	5	6+ 4	2	11+ 1	11+ 6
1	7+ 3	2	4	6	5
4 4	2	11+ 5	6	4+ 3	1

176

9+ 1	3	5	6+ 2	4	6 6
11+ 5	5+ 2	3	10+ 4	6	3+ 1
6	5+ 1	4	6+ 5	5+ 3	2
6+ 4	11+ 5	6	1	2	7+ 3
2	10+ 6	1 1	16+ 3	5	4
3 3	4	2	6	6+ 1	5

177

12+ 4	3	7+ 2	3+ 1	11+ 5	6 6
1	4	5	2	6	4+ 3
6 6	6+ 2	4	8+ 5	3	1
3+ 2	1	10+ 6	7+ 3	9+ 4	5
11+ 5	6	3	4	3+ 1	2
8+ 3	5	1	6 6	6+ 2	4

178

3+ 1	2	3 3	10+ 6	4	14+ 5
5 5	5+ 1	4	8+ 2	6	3
7+ 4	4+ 3	1	9+ 5	3+ 2	6
3	12+ 6	11+ 5	4	1	3+ 2
2	4	6	3 3	12+ 5	1
11+ 6	5	3+ 2	1	3	4

179

11+ 6	**5** 5	**3+** 1	2	**11+** 4	3
5	**13+** 3	**6+** 2	**11+** 6	**3+** 1	4
4+ 3	6	4	5	2	**3+** 1
1	4	**5** 5	**9+** 3	6	2
3+ 2	1	**10+** 6	4	**14+** 3	5
6+ 4	2	**4+** 3	1	**5** 5	6

180

12+ 2	3	**7+** 6	1	**9+** 5	4
3	4	**2** 2	**12+** 5	**8+** 6	**7+** 1
11+ 5	**1** 1	3	4	2	6
6	**9+** 5	4	**3+** 2	1	**3** 3
5+ 1	**11+** 6	5	**13+** 3	4	**10+** 2
4	**3+** 2	1	6	3	5

181

5+ 1	4	**5** 5	**2−** 3	**9+** 6	**8+** 2
2− 4	2	**5−** 1	5	3	6
2− 5	**5−** 1	6	**3+** 2	**7+** 4	3
3	6	**9+** 2	1	**9+** 5	4
11+ 6	5	3	4	**2** 2	**6+** 1
2 2	**1−** 3	4	**5−** 6	1	5

182

3 3	**5−** 1	6	**11+** 2	4	5
11+ 6	**1−** 3	**3+** 2	**4−** 5	1	**13+** 4
5	2	1	**3−** 4	3	6
7+ 4	**11+** 6	**3** 3	1	**10+** 5	2
1	5	**10+** 4	6	**2** 2	3
2	**9+** 4	5	**3** 3	**7+** 6	1

183

17+ 3	5	**1** 1	**10+** 4	6	**12+** 2
4	**6+** 1	2	**8+** 5	3	6
5	3	**5−** 6	1	**3−** 2	4
5− 1	**8+** 6	**6+** 4	2	5	**2−** 3
6	2	**8+** 5	3	**4** 4	1
9+ 2	4	3	**5−** 6	1	**5** 5

184

2− 4	**5−** 6	**2** 2	**12+** 5	**3−** 3	**4−** 1
2	1	3	4	6	5
7+ 3	4	**11+** 6	**5−** 1	**3−** 5	2
5− 1	**3−** 2	5	6	**6+** 4	**13+** 3
6	5	**8+** 1	**3** 3	2	4
5 5	3	4	**3+** 2	1	6

185

1– **3**	7+ **2**	**5**	5– **6**	**1**	4 **4**
2	14+ **5**	**6**	7+ **3**	**4**	5– **1**
11+ **5**	**3**	1 **1**	2– **4**	**2**	**6**
6	5– **1**	2– **4**	4– **5**	5+ **3**	**2**
5+ **4**	**6**	**2**	**1**	8+ **5**	**3**
1	4 **4**	5+ **3**	**2**	1– **6**	**5**

186

3– **3**	11+ **5**	**2**	5– **6**	**1**	4 **4**
6	**4**	11+ **5**	2 **2**	9+ **3**	**1**
5 **5**	5– **1**	**6**	11+ **4**	3– **2**	**3**
7+ **1**	**6**	**4**	**3**	**5**	**2**
2	4+ **3**	**1**	6+ **5**	21+ **4**	**6**
4	1– **2**	**3**	**1**	**6**	**5**

187

8+ 1	3	4	5 5	4− 6	2
3+ 2	1	12+ 3	4	5	14+ 6
4 4	13+ 2	5	6	3+ 1	3
10+ 6	4	1 1	7+ 3	2	5
8+ 5	1− 6	4− 2	1	3	3− 4
3	5	6	6+ 2	4	1

188

4 4	2− 3	5	5− 1	6	3− 2
3+ 1	2	3− 4	11+ 6	9+ 3	5
3− 3	6	1	5	2	4
4− 5	1	3 3	1− 2	10+ 4	6
14+ 6	4	2	3	5 5	4+ 1
2	11+ 5	6	5+ 4	1	3

189

3+ 2	14+ 3	9+ 5	4	5- 1	6
1	6	4 4	10+ 3	5	2
4 4	5	3+ 1	2	9+ 6	3
12+ 5	4	3- 3	6	3+ 2	1
3- 6	1	7+ 2	5	3 3	13+ 4
3	2	5- 6	1	4	5

190

9+ 4	8+ 3	5	3- 1	11+ 6	8+ 2
3	3+ 1	2	4	5	6
2	7+ 4	3	14+ 6	1 1	2- 5
11+ 5	5- 6	1	2	4	3
6	5 5	7+ 4	3	2	3- 1
3+ 1	2	6 6	8+ 5	3	4

191

1− **4**	**3**	5− **1**	**6**	5 **5**	6+ **2**
2 **2**	14+ **6**	**5**	**3**	5+ **1**	**4**
2− **3**	**5**	3+ **2**	**1**	**4**	5− **6**
4− **6**	**2**	9+ **4**	**5**	11+ **3**	**1**
4− **5**	5− **1**	**6**	4 **4**	**2**	2− **3**
1	9+ **4**	**3**	**2**	**6**	**5**

192

3+ **1**	**2**	5− **6**	12+ **5**	**3**	**4**
3− **3**	**6**	**1**	2− **2**	**4**	11+ **5**
3− **4**	**1**	2 **2**	9+ **3**	3− **5**	**6**
11+ **6**	1− **4**	**5**	**1**	**2**	3 **3**
5	**3**	10+ **4**	**6**	3+ **1**	**2**
2 **2**	12+ **5**	**3**	**4**	5− **6**	**1**

193

11+ 5	6	6+ 4	3+ 1	2	7+ 3
3+ 1	3 3	2	11+ 5	6	4
2	2− 5	3	6 6	5+ 4	1
2− 4	2	11+ 5	9+ 3	7+ 1	6
3− 3	5+ 1	6	4	3− 5	2
6	4	1 1	2	2− 3	5

194

3+ 1	2	3 3	15+ 4	5	6
2 2	11+ 6	5	14+ 3	3− 4	3+ 1
11+ 3	4	6	5	1	2
4	3+ 1	2	11+ 6	3	12+ 5
1− 5	4+ 3	1	2	6 6	4
6	9+ 5	4	3+ 1	2	3

195

2 **2**	11+ **6**	**5**	1− **3**	**4**	5− **1**
11+ **3**	**4**	3+ **2**	**1**	4− **5**	**6**
4	8+ **5**	**3**	11+ **6**	**1**	2− **2**
5− **6**	3+ **2**	**1**	**5**	5+ **3**	**4**
1	3 **3**	10+ **6**	**4**	**2**	14+ **5**
10+ **5**	**1**	**4**	2 **2**	**6**	**3**

196

4 **4**	5− **6**	**1**	11+ **5**	3+ **2**	1− **3**
5+ **3**	6+ **5**	4 **4**	**6**	**1**	**2**
2	**1**	11+ **5**	**3**	10+ **4**	**6**
8+ **6**	**2**	**3**	8+ **1**	**5**	10+ **4**
1− **5**	**4**	4− **6**	**2**	3 **3**	**1**
4+ **1**	**3**	**2**	10+ **4**	**6**	**5**

197

6+ 4	2	3− 6	3	7+ 1	5
5+ 3	1− 4	3+ 2	15+ 6	9+ 5	1
2	3	1	5	4	6 6
5− 1	13+ 5	3	4	6 6	9+ 2
6	5− 1	5	2 2	1− 3	4
5 5	6	5+ 4	1	2	3

198

10+ 3	2	5	11+ 1	6	4
6+ 4	11+ 6	3+ 2	7+ 3	5 5	5− 1
2	5	1	4	1− 3	6
11+ 6	1 1	8+ 3	5	4	5+ 2
5	14+ 4	6	3+ 2	1	3
2− 1	3	4	6 6	7+ 2	5

199

8+ 5	**3** 3	**11+** 6	**5−** 1	**11+** 4	**3+** 2
3	**2−** 4	5	6	2	1
5− 1	6	**10+** 3	**2** 2	5	**1−** 4
6	**7+** 2	4	3	**5−** 1	5
6+ 2	5	**1** 1	**12+** 4	6	**3−** 3
4	**3+** 1	2	5	3	6

200

8+ 5	3	**5−** 1	6	**6+** 2	4
9+ 3	**6+** 1	5	**10+** 4	6	**11+** 2
6	**2** 2	**12+** 3	5	4	1
3+ 2	**14+** 6	4	**2−** 3	1	5
1	4	**8+** 6	2	**5** 5	3
11+ 4	5	2	**1** 1	**9+** 3	6